I0425844

July 2012

UNITED NATIONS RENOVATIONS

Best Practices Could Enhance Future Cost Estimates

Accountability ★ Integrity ★ Reliability

GAO Highlights

Highlights of GAO-12-795, a report to congressional requesters

UNITED NATIONS RENOVATIONS

Best Practices Could Enhance Future Cost Estimates

Why GAO Did This Study

In December 2006, the UN approved a $1.88 billion CMP to modernize its headquarters in New York City by 2014, with a scope to include the renovation of five buildings. Separately from the CMP, the UN is also considering the option of a new office building, known as the consolidation building, to be located across the street from UN headquarters. As the UN's largest contributor, the United States has a significant interest in these projects. GAO was asked to report on (1) the extent to which the CMP is meeting its planned renovation scope, schedule, and budget; (2) the UN General Assembly's evaluation of CMP cost estimates; and (3) the status of the consolidation building project.

To perform this work, GAO reviewed cost and schedule documents for the CMP, as well as planning and legal documents for the consolidation building; examined relevant UN financial documents and UN General Assembly resolutions, as well as GAO's best practices for cost estimation; and met with officials from the Department of State (State), the UN CMP office and other relevant UN departments, and New York City.

What GAO Recommends

The Secretary of State and the U.S. Permanent Representative to the United Nations should work with other member states to direct the CMP office and the UN to utilize best practices identified by GAO when developing cost estimates for the CMP and the consolidation building. State and the UN concurred with GAO's recommendations.

View GAO-12-795. For more information, contact Thomas Melito at (202) 512-9601 or melitot@gao.gov, or David Wise at (202) 512-2834 or wised@gao.gov.

What GAO Found

The Capital Master Plan (CMP) has made progress, but may not deliver the project's original scope, faces risks meeting its scheduled completion date, and is projected to be about $430 million over budget as of February 2012. Regarding the project's scope, the CMP office may not renovate the Library and South Annex—two of the five buildings in its original scope—due to the lack of a workable design solution to address security concerns. Related to schedule, the CMP office expects to complete the CMP in 2014, but reports that previous schedule delays have reduced its ability to respond to unforeseen events without affecting the project's end date. According to the CMP office, the project's approximately $430 million in projected cost overruns are due to a number of factors, including about $266 million in direct project costs and over $164 million from scope additions authorized without a corresponding increase in budget by the United Nations (UN) General Assembly. The CMP office has proposed financing options that could address a portion of these cost overruns. However, even if approved, an additional member assessment may be needed. One option for funding the U.S. portion of an additional member assessment is the use of credits attributable to the United States in the UN Tax Equalization Fund (TEF)—a fund used to reimburse U.S. nationals working at the UN for taxes paid on their UN salaries. According to the UN, as of May 2012, the balance of TEF credits attributable to the United States stood at $120.9 million.

After evaluating the CMP's cost estimates, the UN General Assembly issued a resolution in April 2012 stating that the estimates lacked transparency, timeliness, and clarity. For example, the UN General Assembly expressed concern about the lack of clarity regarding the renovation of the Library and South Annex buildings. Specifically, member states inquired about the schedule for the two buildings and why renovations to the buildings were delayed. To address these concerns, the UN General Assembly requested that the CMP office improve reporting on projected CMP cost increases. While the UN General Assembly resolution did not specifically identify how the CMP office should report its future cost estimates, GAO has identified best practices for high-quality and reliable cost estimates. For instance, a well-documented cost estimate should describe in detail how the estimate was developed and the methodology used. Applying these best practices, as appropriate, could address the concerns raised by the UN General Assembly regarding the CMP's cost estimates.

To address its future office space needs, the UN is considering the option of a new building that would be separate from the CMP, but it does not have an estimate of the project's costs. The UN estimates that by 2023 its office space needs will have exceeded the capacity of its current real estate portfolio, primarily due to expiring leases. As a potential solution, the City and State of New York have proposed the construction of a new building known as the consolidation building. The UN has indicated its willingness to consider this proposal, but has not entered into any formal agreements. The current lack of a cost estimate for the consolidation building makes its cost implications for the UN and its member states unclear. GAO has previously reported that cost estimates are critical to program success, such as informed resource investments.

_____ United States Government Accountability Office

Contents

Figures

Abbreviations

CMP	Capital Master Plan
State	Department of State
TEF	Tax Equalization Fund
UN	United Nations
UNDC	United Nations Development Corporation
USUN	U.S. Mission to the United Nations

This is a work of the U.S. government and is not subject to copyright protection in the United States. The published product may be reproduced and distributed in its entirety without further permission from GAO. However, because this work may contain copyrighted images or other material, permission from the copyright holder may be necessary if you wish to reproduce this material separately.

United States Government Accountability Office
Washington, DC 20548

July 25, 2012

The Honorable Richard G. Lugar
Ranking Member
Committee on Foreign Relations
United States Senate

The Honorable Susan M. Collins
Ranking Member
Committee on Homeland Security and Governmental Affairs
United States Senate

The Honorable Ileana Ros-Lehtinen
Chairman
Committee on Foreign Affairs
House of Representatives

In December 2006, the United Nations (UN) approved a $1.88 billion Capital Master Plan (CMP) to renovate and modernize its headquarters complex by 2014.[1] To support the CMP, the United States has provided approximately $388 million in assessed contributions to the UN. In addition to the $388 million, $100 million in UN credits attributable to the United States were also used to support the project. Renovations to the UN headquarters complex began in 2008. We have periodically reviewed UN efforts to develop and implement the CMP and reported on the progress of the project.[2] In our most recent report in 2009, we reported that the CMP was on schedule, but $97.5 million over budget, and that the UN was considering adding $206.6 million in related costs to the CMP without a corresponding increase in budget.[3] Since 2009, the UN has reported continued cost overruns associated with the CMP.

---

[1]G.A. Res. 61/251, UN GAOR, 61st Sess., UN Doc. A/RES/61/251 (2006).

[2]For a list of previous reports we have issued on the planning and progress of the CMP, see Related GAO Products at the end of this report.

[3]GAO, *United Nations: Renovation Still Scheduled for Completion in 2013, but Risks to Its Schedule and Cost Remain*, GAO-09-870R (Washington, D.C.: July 30, 2009). When we reported in July 2009, the CMP was scheduled to be completed in 2013.

Separately from the CMP, the UN General Assembly[4] has stressed the need for a long-term strategy to meet the office space needs of the UN.[5] The UN leases over 2 million square feet of office space in multiple locations in New York City. In 2011, the City and State of New York authorized the construction of a new office building for UN personnel to be located across the street from the UN headquarters complex. This building, known as the consolidation building, would allow the UN to consolidate a portion of its personnel from leased space in various locations in New York City into one office building. While the project is still in its early stages, the United States, as the largest contributor to the UN, has significant financial interest in whether this project proceeds.

This report provides information on the progress of the CMP and the status of the UN consolidation building. Specifically, we examine (1) the extent to which the CMP is meeting its planned renovation scope, schedule, and budget; (2) the UN General Assembly's evaluation of CMP cost estimates; and (3) the status of the consolidation building project.

To evaluate the extent to which the CMP is meeting its planned renovation scope, schedule, and budget, we analyzed CMP planning, schedule, and budget documents to compare current planned scope, completion dates, and cost estimates to initial scope, schedule, and budget projections. Further, we examined other relevant CMP documentation, including information on risk assessments, monthly reports, and procurement information. We also reviewed financing proposals reported by the CMP office, the Financial Rules and Regulations of the UN, and UN Financial Reports and Audited Financial Statements. To examine the UN General Assembly's evaluation of CMP cost estimates, we reviewed and analyzed CMP documents describing the project's financial condition as of February 2012 presented to the UN's Fifth Committee, which covers budget and administrative issues, as well as UN General Assembly resolutions pertaining to the CMP. We also analyzed how best practices for cost estimating from our *Cost Estimating and Assessment Guide* could potentially address issues raised by the UN

---

[4]The General Assembly is the UN's main policy-making body and comprises all 193 member states.

[5]G.A. Res. 60/282, UN GAOR, 60th Sess., UN Doc A/RES/60/282 (2006).

General Assembly regarding CMP cost information.[6] For these objectives, we also interviewed officials from the Department of State (State) and relevant UN offices, including the CMP office, Program Planning and Budget Division, Board of Auditors, and Office of Internal Oversight Services, as well as toured the CMP project site. To assess the status of the consolidation building project we reviewed planning and legal documents. We also interviewed officials from State, relevant UN offices, the UN Development Corporation, and the City of New York regarding plans for and the estimated cost of the consolidation building. Additional information about our scope and methodology is provided in appendix I.

We conducted our work from January 2012 to July 2012 in accordance with generally accepted government auditing standards. Those standards require that we plan and perform our work to obtain sufficient, appropriate evidence to provide a reasonable basis for our findings and conclusions based on our objectives. We believe that the evidence obtained provides a reasonable basis for our findings and conclusions based on our objectives.

Background

Original Budget, Financing, Schedule, and Scope of the CMP

In 2001, we reported that the UN headquarters complex in New York City—built largely between 1949 to 1952[7]—no longer conformed to current safety, fire, and building codes or to UN technology and security requirements.[8] The UN General Assembly noted that conditions in the UN headquarters complex posed serious risks to the health and safety of staff, visitors, and tourists. Thus, in December 2006, after several years of design and planning, the UN General Assembly unanimously approved the CMP to renovate the UN headquarters complex, at a budget not to exceed $1.88 billion.

---

[6]GAO, *Cost Estimating and Assessment Guide*, GAO-09-3SP (Washington, D.C.: Mar. 2009).

[7]Additional buildings in the complex, such as the Library and South Annex, were built between 1960 and 1982.

[8]GAO, *United Nations: Planning for Headquarters Renovation is Reasonable; United States Needs to Decide Whether to Support Work*, GAO-01-788 (Washington, D.C.: June 15, 2001).

To finance the CMP, the UN General Assembly approved a strategy to assess member states for the cost of the CMP, under which they could choose to pay their assessment in either a lump sum or over a 5-year period, from 2007 to 2011. CMP assessments, whether collected as lump-sum or multi-year payments, were invested to earn interest income. The UN General Assembly also approved a $45 million working capital reserve to cover any temporary cash flow deficits. According to the CMP office, member states would receive this reserve back in the form of a credit at the end of the project's construction phase. The United States chose to pay its assessment for the CMP in five equal payments of $75.5 million per year starting in 2007, for a total of approximately $378 million. The United States also paid a separate assessment to the project's working capital reserve of about $9.9 million in 2007. In the resolution approving the CMP, the UN General Assembly decided that, in the event of cost escalations over the approved budget of $1.88 billion, member states would be subject to a further assessment to meet the revised requirements of the CMP.

The UN General Assembly approved the completion of the CMP's scope during the scheduled period of 2006 to 2014. This scope included the renovation of five buildings on the UN headquarters complex—the General Assembly Building, the Conference Building, the Secretariat Building, the Library, and the South Annex—as well as renovation of the basements connecting several of those buildings and the construction of a temporary conference building on the North Lawn of the complex. Figure 1 shows the existing buildings of the UN headquarters complex, along with the temporary conference building.

Source: GAO and United Nations.

To house UN staff during the renovation, the CMP included plans to lease swing space in nearby buildings. Additionally, the CMP included landscaping, demolition of the temporary conference building, additional blast protection, measures to promote environmental sustainability, and improvements to the reliability and redundancy of headquarters systems such as emergency power.

Changes to the CMP Authorized by the UN General Assembly: 2006-2009

In several resolutions, the UN General Assembly noted that it has the sole prerogative to decide on any changes to the CMP's scope, budget, and implementation strategy. Since December 2006, the UN General Assembly has exercised this prerogative to make changes to the CMP or authorize changes proposed by the Secretary-General. These changes include:

- *Accelerated Strategy IV*: In December 2007, the UN General Assembly approved an expedited strategy for the CMP known as accelerated strategy IV. This approach approved the renovation to proceed in two concurrent phases: one to renovate the Secretariat Building and one to renovate the Conference Building, General Assembly Building, and other buildings. Under the previous approach, the UN had planned on renovating buildings in multiple phases, including renovating the Secretariat Building while it was 75 percent occupied. The accelerated strategy called for the temporary relocation of most of the staff of the Secretariat Building during the renovation—which required the CMP office to increase the amount of leased swing space—and expedited the schedule for the Secretariat Building's renovation by reducing construction time from 6 to 3 years. The strategy also affected the schedules for the construction of the temporary conference building, as well as the renovation of the Conference Building and General Assembly Building. The CMP office reported that such an implementation strategy would reduce risks associated with the CMP. The CMP office also estimated that the strategy would produce an estimated cost overrun of $190 million, which it would seek to reduce through the process of value engineering.[9]

- *Associated Costs*: In April 2009, the UN General Assembly decided that certain costs related to the CMP—known as associated costs—would be financed from within the $1.88 billion CMP budget.[10] Associated costs cover a wide range of requirements, such as broadcast equipment, new furniture, and additional staffing requirements to manage information technology and security.[11] According to CMP officials, these costs were originally expected to be funded by UN program offices through the regular UN budget process. Therefore, the CMP office's original cost estimates for the CMP did not include new furniture or equipment except where the equipment was part of the permanent infrastructure of the UN. For instance, according to the CMP office, the original CMP scope only provided for furniture for three new mid-sized conference rooms and supplemental office furniture associated with swing spaces. While associated costs are funded from within the CMP budget, UN departments other than the CMP office manage these costs. For example, the UN Department of Safety and Security manages costs

---

[9]Value engineering is the process of reviewing a project's objectives and design, and finding ways to achieve the same objectives at a lower cost. In February 2009, the CMP office informed the UN Advisory Committee on Administrative and Budgetary Questions that the decision to renovate the Conference Building in a single phase was the most significant change to the scope of the project resulting from value engineering. The Committee noted that some of the savings identified by the CMP office through value engineering actually resulted from external, market-related factors.

[10]The resolution also noted that the CMP office entered into commitments for associated costs absent the formal approval of the UN General Assembly.

[11]Other associated costs requirements include moving supplies and services, archive space, and storage facilities.

related to security. Prior to the UN General Assembly's decision on associated costs, the CMP office reported that the CMP budget could not absorb associated costs without exceeding $1.88 billion. However, the UN General Assembly argued that the CMP office could realize further cost reductions that would enable the CMP to absorb associated costs.

- *Secondary Data Center.* In April 2009, the UN General Assembly requested that the CMP partially absorb costs associated with a secondary data center, including leasing a commercial facility and establishing a service delivery agreement to provide equipment and services. The secondary data center serves as a backup system to enable the UN to respond to emergency situations that may impair operations of critical elements of its information and communications technology infrastructure and facilities. In resolutions in April 2009 and December 2009, the UN General Assembly requested that the CMP budget absorb $16.7 million to fund the secondary data center.[12]

Progress Made on CMP, but Two Building Renovations May Not Be Completed and Project Is Projected to Be Approximately $430 Million over Budget

While the CMP nears completion of the renovation of two of the five buildings, the project has suspended the originally planned renovation of two buildings, faces risks meeting its 2014 completion date, and is projected to be approximately $430 million over budget. The CMP office may not renovate two buildings that were originally part of the scope of the project, due to the lack of a workable design solution to address security requirements. In addition, the CMP office predicts that it will complete the CMP by the end of 2014, but risks, such as a compressed schedule with work yet to be contracted, exist. Moreover, as of February 2012, the CMP office estimates that the project will be about $430 million over its approved budget of $1.88 billion—an increase of approximately 53 percent (approximately $149 million) from its last reported estimate. According to the CMP office, a number of factors, such as unforeseen conditions and complexities in the basements and Conference Building, contributed to the increase in projected cost overruns. The CMP office has proposed options to address a portion of these cost overruns; however, even if approved, additional funding will be needed to address the remainder. The United States could potentially use credits it has with the UN to fund an assessment related to the CMP.

---

[12]The UN General Assembly also requested that the support account for peacekeeping operations absorb approximately $4.2 million in costs associated with the secondary data center.

Progress Made on CMP Renovations

The CMP office has nearly completed the first two building renovations of the CMP—the Secretariat and Conference Buildings—which began in 2010. By February 2013, both buildings are scheduled to be completely renovated and back in use. Specifically, the CMP office plans for the Secretariat Building to be primarily reoccupied and in use by November 2012. The CMP office predicts completion of the renovation of the Conference Building by the end of 2012, with the building reoccupied and in use in February 2013. The CMP office has reported a number of other achievements of the CMP, such as:

- Modernizing 1 million square feet in the basements, including installation of chilled water piping, electrical conduit and wire, telecommunication conduit and copper cable.

- Redesigning the Conference Building to take into account enhanced security upgrades.[13] According to the CMP office, the enhanced security upgrades include two major activities: structurally enhancing the Conference Building and associated basements to withstand blast threats and installing protective structures, including bollards and gates, along the perimeter of the UN complex. The CMP office anticipates that the enhanced security upgrades will be completed by 2014.

- Substantially completing the removal and replacement of the glass curtain wall in the Secretariat Building, shown in figure 2.

---

[13]The United States and the UN reached an agreement in January 2011 on the design requirements for more stringent security measures than those originally planned for the CMP. In 2010, the CMP office, in consultation with the UN Department of Safety and Security, undertook additional studies to examine the effect on UN facilities of potential vehicle-borne explosive devices. As a result of these studies, the UN decided to implement enhanced security upgrades for the CMP. The United States did not object to the UN's use of up to $100 million in credits attributable to the United States from the UN Tax Equalization Fund to fund the upgrades. Noting this funding, the UN General Assembly decided that the costs related to the enhanced security upgrades would not be recovered through an assessment imposed on member states.

GAO-12-795 UN Renovations

Figure 2: Glass Curtain Wall of the Secretariat Building, as of May 2012

Source: CMP office.

The UN General Assembly has requested that the CMP office provide information on contracts awarded for the CMP. The CMP office posts information on contract awards on the UN Procurement Division and CMP websites. According to the CMP office, 85 percent of the value of CMP contracts has gone to U.S. firms.

Renovations for Two Buildings May Not Be Completed

Security requirements and concerns have led the CMP office to suspend originally planned renovations for two buildings—the Library and the South Annex. In 2010, UN security studies found these buildings to be vulnerable to vehicle blast threats. As of April 2012, CMP officials stated that they lacked a workable design solution to address these security concerns. Specifically, according to CMP officials, the only solution to the risk of blast threats would be to close a nearby highway exit ramp.[14] However, based on discussions between the UN and the United States,

[14]In October 2011, the CMP office reported that the options regarding the future of the Library and South Annex were (1) moving the off-ramp, (2) closing the off-ramp, (3) closing the Library and South Annex upon completion of the CMP, or (4) assuming that no solution would be found and demolishing the buildings.

the CMP office does not view this outcome as likely. To renovate the Library and South Annex to the required security standards, CMP officials told us that they would have to demolish the buildings and begin new construction. CMP officials also told us that since they do not have a viable renovation option for these buildings, they have not updated their initial design and cost estimates. Absent a solution to the security vulnerabilities of the Library and South Annex, CMP officials told us that only limited use of the buildings would be possible. In May 2012, the CMP office reported that it plans to consult with UN departments affected by the suspension to determine where to relocate functions impacted by potentially not renovating the buildings.

CMP Office Projects 2014 Completion, but Risks to Schedule Exist

The CMP office expects to complete the CMP by 2014, but its schedule faces risks, such as a compressed schedule with some work yet to be contracted. As of February 2012, the CMP office estimates completing renovations by mid-2014, about 1 year behind the schedule it reported in October 2008. As shown in table 1, while the completion date for the project is still estimated to be mid-2014, the projected completion dates for key CMP activities have experienced delays for various reasons.

Table 1: Projected Completion Dates for Key CMP Activities

Activity	Date as of October 2008 (Accelerated Strategy IV)	Date as of February 2012	Approximate delay of	Reasons for delays
Basements	Early 2011[a]	Mid-2014	39 months	Delayed due to unexpected complexities in basement conditions.
Conference Building	Mid-2011	Late 2012	15 months	Delayed due to enhanced security upgrades.
Secretariat Building	Early 2012	Mid-2012	3 months	Delayed due to the delay in the construction of the temporary conference building.
Library	Early 2013	————	————	Suspended pending resolution of the security issue.
General Assembly Building	Mid-2013	Mid-2014	12 months	Delayed due to enhanced security upgrades to the Conference Building.[b]
South Annex	Early 2012	————	————	Suspended pending resolution of the security issue.
Completion of CMP Activities	**Mid-2013**	**Mid-2014**	**12 months**	

Source: GAO analysis of CMP data.

[a]The CMP office did not report a completion date for the basements as of October 2008. We have included the completion date reported in the original schedule as of October 2006.

[b]According to the CMP office, it cannot begin renovations to the General Assembly Building until it completes renovations to the Conference Building.

CMP officials attribute schedule delays mostly to enhanced security upgrades added to the CMP in 2011. We reported in 2009 that security upgrades to the CMP represented a key risk to the project's progress.[15] According to the CMP office, implementing enhanced security upgrades to address security issues resulted in a delay of about 1 year in the schedule of the Conference Building. Although it reported a mid-2011 completion date as of October 2008, the CMP office now estimates that the Conference Building renovation will be completed in late 2012.

According to the CMP office, despite delayed start dates for a number of activities, the CMP office has maintained a 2014 project completion date. However, the CMP office faces two key risks related to meeting this date:

---

[15]GAO-09-870R. The CMP office's risk register identified the risk of security upgrades to the CMP as having a low probability of occurring, but a significant impact if it did occur.

- *Compressed schedule.* CMP officials noted that maintaining the 2014 project completion date while experiencing delays to the start dates for several projects has created a compressed schedule, which reduces the ability to develop workaround solutions if problems arise. For example, CMP officials identified the completion of the Conference Building renovation as a "critical path" of the project's schedule, because renovations to the General Assembly Building cannot begin until those to the Conference Building are completed. Once the CMP office moves conference functions back into the Conference Building, it will reconfigure the temporary conference building to house the functions of the General Assembly Building while the General Assembly Building undergoes renovation. Previously, as a result of delays in the Conference Building's schedule, the CMP office delayed the completion date of the General Assembly Building from mid-2013 to mid-2014. CMP officials said that the amount of time that the Conference Building renovation can be delayed without impacting the overall project's completion date is minimal.

- *Work yet to be contracted.* The CMP office has yet to contract work for various remaining parts of the project and thus does not have agreed upon completion dates with the contractors that will be doing the work. For instance, as of March 2012, the CMP office reported that it had not committed any funds for the renovation of the General Assembly Building. CMP officials told us that conditions in the General Assembly Building—such as the potential for asbestos and weaknesses in the building's concrete slab—also constitute potential risks. Additionally, the CMP has not fully contracted for renovation work in the basements. CMP officials have noted that renovation in the basements is linked to the overall renovations, as the basements house the infrastructure for the UN complex. CMP officials have described the work in this area as highly complex and have noted that to date it has taken longer than expected.

Projected Total CMP Cost Overruns Approximately $430 Million

As of February 2012, the CMP office projected total cost overruns of about $430 million over the CMP's approved budget of $1.88 billion.[16] According to the CMP office, the estimated cost overruns result from a number of factors, including about $266 million in direct project costs and about $164 million in scope additions authorized by the UN General Assembly to be financed from within the project's approved budget, as shown in table 2.

Table 2: Factors Contributing to CMP's Projected Cost Overruns of Approximately $430 Million, as of February 2012

Dollars in millions

Category	Description	Estimate	Percent of total
Direct costs of the CMP	• Includes renovation costs, swing space estimates, contingency, and price escalation. Renovation costs include construction, professional fees, and management costs.	$265.7	62.0
Associated costs	• In April 2009, the UN General Assembly decided that associated costs would be financed from within the $1.88 billion CMP budget. • The estimate for associated costs covers the period of 2008 to 2013. The majority of the associated costs relate to the renovation of the Secretariat Building and the Conference Building, with the main cost drivers pertaining to the purchase of furniture and the permanent broadcast facility and media asset management system.	146.8	34.0
Secondary data center	• In April 2009, the UN General Assembly requested that the CMP partially absorb costs associated with a secondary data center. • The costs of the secondary data center are shared between the regular budget and the peacekeeping support account—80 percent to 20 percent, respectively—on the basis of the proportion of capacity used. The CMP office finances the 80 percent share.	17.4[a]	4.0

Source: GAO analysis of CMP office data and UN General Assembly resolutions.

[a]The total estimated cost for the secondary data center is $20.7 million, with costs shared between the CMP budget and peacekeeping support account. The total cost funded by the CMP budget, as of February 2012, is $17.4 million. The UN General Assembly requested that the support account for peacekeeping operations absorb approximately $4.2 million in costs associated with the secondary data center. The CMP office has received about $3.3 million and expects to receive another $0.9 million from the peacekeeping support account to fund the secondary data center.

[16]The total cost overrun estimate includes a combination of accrued costs for work already completed and projected costs for work not yet contracted. For example, the CMP has awarded large contracts for ongoing work in the Conference Building, Secretariat Building, and basements. As a result, some portions of the total projected cost overruns for the CMP, such as swing space and asbestos costs, are actual costs. However, the estimated cost overruns also include a number of projected costs, such as those for the General Assembly Building, where the CMP office has yet to award contracts.

Projected CMP cost overruns increased significantly between May 2011 and February 2012.[17] The UN General Assembly described the increase as "sudden and unexplained." In October 2011, the CMP office reported that it had committed 84.5 percent of the CMP funding against the original $1.88 billion budget, which significantly reduced the risk of unexpected, adverse events during the remainder of the project.[18] As shown in table 3, estimated cost overruns increased by approximately 53 percent (roughly $149 million) between May 2011 and February 2012, driven primarily by direct costs to the CMP.

[17]The CMP reported cost estimates as of May 2011 in its ninth annual progress report on the CMP, which was published in October 2011.

[18]The CMP office reported similar information in 2009 when changing its budget reporting by combining the cost estimates for contingency and escalation. The CMP office reported that it combined the accounts because it had less uncertainty about the timing and risks of the project. Similarly, in September 2007, in remarking on accelerated strategy IV, the CMP office reported that it would know almost all of the contract values within the first 3 years of the project, greatly reducing the financial risks to the UN.

GAO-12-795 UN Renovations

Table 3: CMP Cost Estimates

Dollars in millions

Category	As of May 2011	As of February 2012	Change
Direct costs to the CMP[a]	$2,004.5	$2,153.5	$149.1
Associated costs	146.8	146.8	-
Enhanced security upgrades[b]	99.6	99.6	-
Secondary data center	20.7	20.7	-
Total costs	2,271.5	2,420.6	149.1
Less			
UN General Assembly approved budget and other funding[c]	1,990.5	1,990.7	0.2
Total projected cost overruns	**281.0**	**429.9**	**148.9**

Source: GAO analysis of CMP office data.

[a]Direct costs to the CMP include costs for CMP swing space rent after October 2012.

[b]The CMP received "up to" $100 million to fund the enhanced security upgrades. While the CMP reports $99.6 million in costs for these updates, it applies the entire $100 million as part of its available funding. As a result, the total projected cost overruns are understated by $0.4 million.

[c]Other funding includes voluntary contributions, $100 million to fund enhanced security upgrades, and $3.3 million in funding from the peacekeeping support account to support the secondary data center. A $0.2 million increase in voluntary contributions accounts for the difference between the amount of funds in May 2011 and February 2012.

Although the increase in estimated cost overruns reported in February 2012 are attributable to the direct costs of the CMP, a portion consists of costs added to the CMP over time by the UN General Assembly without a corresponding increase in the CMP budget—such as associated costs and the secondary data center. CMP officials told us that they assume responsibility for direct costs of the CMP—which include renovation, swing space, contingency, and escalation—but have no control over additional related costs added to the CMP. In explaining the reasons for the estimated cost overruns directly attributable to the project, the CMP office cited several factors, including the following:

- *Asbestos abatement.* According to the CMP office, when the renovations began, the volume of asbestos found far exceeded its expectations. Moreover, new regulations enacted by New York City in 2010 made the abatement of that asbestos even more complicated and expensive.

- *Unforeseen conditions in the Conference Building.* The CMP office reported that the actual construction of the concrete floor slabs in the Conference Building differed from the original design drawings. The construction of the concrete floor slabs required the CMP office to amend the design of the Conference Building. As of March 2012, the CMP office reported that it expected to find similar conditions in the General Assembly Building.

- *Complexities in the basements.* The CMP office noted that work in the basements was more complex than expected due, in part, to limited documentation of the basement infrastructure and relocation of essential mechanical systems. For instance, the CMP office reported that UN documentation did not account for the large quantity of existing telephone, electrical, and security cables in the ceilings of the basements. According to the CMP office, each of these cables had to be individually tested to ensure that the CMP office did not remove active infrastructure, which was a labor-intensive process. Figure 3 shows examples of ceiling conditions in the basements before and after CMP renovations.

Figure 3: Ceiling Conditions in the Basement of a UN Building before and after Renovation

Source: CMP office.

Proposals to Address Cost Overruns Exist, but New Member Assessment May Be Needed

To address cost overruns of the CMP, the CMP office recommended that the UN General Assembly endorse two financing proposals. Specifically, the CMP office proposed utilizing the working capital reserve fund and the interest income on CMP funds. As of February 2012, $45 million was available in the working capital reserve fund and the interest income amounted to $107.2 million. As of May 2012, the UN General Assembly had not made a decision to approve the use of these funds, but the Advisory Committee on Administrative and Budgetary Questions had reviewed and supported the proposals.[19] If the UN General Assembly approves the utilization of the working capital reserve fund and the interest income, these funds will cover about a third of the projected cost overruns, but cost overruns in the amount of approximately $277.7 million will still not be addressed.

The CMP office is also exploring options to further address estimated cost overruns by not fully renovating two buildings included in the original CMP renovation scope. With no solution to the security issues related to the Library and South Annex, CMP officials told us that they would propose limiting the scope of the renovations to these buildings. Rather than renovating as originally planned, the renovations to the Library and South Annex would only include connecting them to new building systems, such as heating and air conditioning. Based on the original cost estimate for these buildings, the CMP office estimates that not fully renovating the two buildings would eliminate $65 million in planned work, which could be applied to address projected cost overruns of the CMP. CMP officials also told us that they plan to explore additional opportunities to reduce work and achieve savings related to site landscaping and the General Assembly Building, but have not estimated the potential savings of these options. As shown in table 4, combining the proposed financing options with reductions in the project's planned scope would still leave the project with a shortfall of $212.7 million.

---

[19]Although the UN General Assembly did not make a decision on whether the CMP office could utilize the working capital reserve or interest income in the March 2012 resumed session, the General Assembly did authorize the Secretary-General to enter into commitments of up to an additional $135 million for resources required for the CMP project through 2012. The UN General Assembly did not identify a source of funding for the $135 million in new commitment authority for the CMP. According to UN officials, the eventual funding could be sourced through the use of the working capital reserve and interest income on the CMP, or it could be sourced from an assessment on member states.

Table 4: Estimated CMP Cost Overruns after Utilizing Financing Options and Proposed Reductions in Project Scope, as of February 2012

Dollars in millions

Category	Estimate
Projected cost overruns of the CMP	$429.9
Working capital reserve	(45.0)
Interest income from CMP funds	(107.2)
Reduction in renovation scope of Library and South Annex	(65.0)
Total estimated CMP cost overruns	**212.7**

Source: GAO analysis of CMP office data.

Another potential financing option is an additional member assessment. In the resolution approving the CMP, the UN General Assembly decided that, in the event of cost escalations over the approved budget of $1.88 billion, member states would be subject to a further assessment to meet the revised requirements of the CMP. The actual amount of such an assessment would depend on the decisions of the UN General Assembly regarding proposed financing and reduced scope options. The U.S. share of any future assessment would be 22 percent.

One potential option for funding all or part of an additional U.S. member assessment for the CMP would be using credits in the UN Tax Equalization Fund (TEF) account—a UN fund used to reimburse U.S. nationals working at the UN for U.S. taxes paid on their UN salaries. (For more information on the UN TEF, see appendix II.) According to the UN, as of December 31, 2011, there was a balance of $134 million in TEF credits attributable to the United States. This balance remained after the UN applied $100 million in TEF credits attributable to the United States to fund the enhanced security upgrades to the CMP in 2011. Congress has since passed legislation related to the use of TEF credits. The Consolidated Appropriations Act of 2012, passed in December 2011, required that TEF credits shall only be available for the United States' assessed contributions to the UN and shall be subject to the regular notification procedures of the Committees on Appropriations.[20] State told

---

[20]Pub. Law No. 112-74, 125 Stat. 1168.

us that it is complying with these provisions.[21] For instance, in January 2012, the U.S. Mission to the UN requested that the UN apply $13.1 million of TEF credits attributable to the United States toward the United States' regular UN budget assessment for calendar year 2011. After the application of these credits, the balance of TEF credits attributable to the United States stood at $120.9 million, as of May 2012. However, under this policy, TEF credits could be used to fund cost overruns of the CMP if the cost overruns are funded through a member assessment as called for by the resolution approving the CMP.

Use of Best Practices May Address UN General Assembly Concerns Regarding CMP Cost Estimates

In April 2012, the UN General Assembly issued a resolution expressing concerns regarding the transparency, timeliness, and clarity of the CMP's February 2012 cost estimates. To address these concerns, the UN General Assembly requested that the CMP office improve reporting on the underlying causes of the projected CMP cost increases. While the UN General Assembly resolution did not specifically identify how the CMP office should report its future cost estimates, we have identified best practices associated with high-quality and reliable cost estimates. Applying these best practices, as appropriate, may address the UN General Assembly's concerns regarding CMP cost estimates.

UN General Assembly Has Expressed Concerns Regarding CMP Cost Estimates

After evaluating the CMP office's February 2012 cost information, the UN General Assembly reported a number of concerns with these estimates, such as a lack of transparency, timeliness, and clarity. For example, with regard to transparency, member states inquired why the CMP office did not include $38 million in increased swing space leasing costs in earlier CMP cost estimates. The CMP office noted that it negotiated swing space leases for a period longer than necessary to mitigate the risk of CMP schedule delays. The CMP office did not include these costs in its earlier estimates because it assumed these leases could be terminated early or

---

[21]It is unclear whether these provisions are relevant to the use of existing TEF credits attributable to the United States. According to State, once the United States provides assessed contributions to the UN, the organization legally controls them. While State officials said that the UN generally weighs U.S. preferences regarding the use of TEF credits it has contributed to the organization, ultimately the use of these credits is at the sole discretion of the UN. However, State officials told us that they will not endorse the use by the UN of TEF credits attributable to the United States for any purpose other than assessed contributions and that it is unlikely that the UN would act unilaterally to use TEF credits for a purpose to which State objected. UN officials confirmed this statement.

used by other UN departments in the event the CMP project no longer needed the swing space. According to the CMP office, in a healthy rental market, early termination or subleasing is common; however, the economic downturn prevented it from taking such actions. In addition, member states inquired about the main factors that led to the projected increase in cost overruns. According to the CMP office, a key factor of the projected cost overruns was increased asbestos abatement costs related to asbestos found in the basements and Conference Building in late 2011. However, the CMP office had previously reported that all asbestos was abated from Conference Rooms 1-3 of the Conference Building in February 2011. Further, the 2011 CMP annual report considered the abatement of asbestos and the removal of obsolete materials from the Secretariat and Conference Buildings a significant achievement. For additional information regarding the concerns of the UN General Assembly and issues raised by member states, see table 5.

Table 5: UN General Assembly Concerns, Specific Issues Raised, and Additional Information Related to the CMP February 2012 Cost Updates

Concern expressed by the UN General Assembly	Specific issues raised	Additional information
Lack of transparency and timely information on budget, forecasts, and projected cost overruns	• The factors that led to the increase in cost overruns of the CMP.	• The CMP office provided qualitative explanations of the differences between planned and actual costs for major renovation activities, such as buildings and swing space. However, it did not quantify individual cost drivers for major renovation activities, nor did it clearly identify what parts of its estimates were based on actual versus projected costs.
	• The original budget for swing space rent.	• The CMP office reported a budgeted swing space estimate of $464 million, as of February 2012. However, this estimate is $74 million higher than what the CMP office reported when it proposed accelerated strategy IV in 2007.
Lack of transparency and timely information on risks	• The volume, value, and reasons for change orders within the CMP.	• The CMP office presented information on the reasons for change orders, such as field conditions. Member states expressed interest in more details, such as which UN departments requested changes. Moreover, the UN Board of Auditors reported that the CMP office cost estimate did not include a robustly calculated estimate for the cost of all change orders.
	• The potential for costs of the enhanced security upgrades to exceed the budgeted projection.	• The CMP office reported that it does not expect any cost overruns for the enhanced security upgrades. However, the CMP office reports that it is developing a total cost estimate and awaiting approval for portions of the upgrades. The UN Board of Auditors reported that the cost of enhanced security upgrades is high-risk, given third party approvals.
Lack of clarity regarding the renovation of the Library and South Annex	• The cost estimates, delayed schedules, and prospective plans for the Library and South Annex.	• The CMP office reported that reducing the scope of the renovations to the Library and South Annex would result in an estimated $65 million savings. However, the UN Board of Auditors has reported that the original budgets for the CMP do not clearly identify the costs for these buildings.

Source: GAO analysis based on information provided by the CMP office and UN General Assembly resolution A/RES/66/258.

Officials from the U.S. Mission to the UN (USUN) also raised concerns with the explanation of the projected CMP cost overruns, both during and at the conclusion of the March 2012 session. For example, a U.S. representative at the March 2012 session asked about the amount and utilization of the remaining contingency fund for the CMP. While the CMP office reported that $89.1 million remained in funds for contingency and price escalation, this amount was as of May 2011, before the increase in estimated cost overruns reported in March 2012.[22] Moreover, USUN officials told us that despite the briefings and information provided by the CMP office, there was still insufficient information as to why and when the projected cost overruns occurred.[23]

While CMP officials told us that they could not currently quantify the individual cost drivers of the $149 million increase in projected cost overruns that occurred between May 2011 and February 2012, they stated that the February 2012 estimates were the best available. Further, they noted that it is difficult to attribute the causes for cost overruns to specific buildings. For example, asbestos abatement is a campus-wide activity that affects the cost of all building renovations.

After evaluating CMP cost estimates, the UN General Assembly issued a resolution in April 2012 requesting that the CMP office produce additional reporting related to CMP costs. Specifically, the UN General Assembly requested more information on the underlying causes of the projected cost increases and practical options to address them.

Use of Best Practices in Future CMP Cost Reporting May Address UN General Assembly Concerns

While the UN General Assembly resolution did not explicitly identify how the CMP office should report future cost information, we have found that a high-quality and reliable cost estimate should exhibit certain best practices, including being comprehensive, well-documented, accurate, and credible.[24] These best practices include elements for documenting and reporting cost estimates. For example, a cost estimate that is well-documented and accurate should allow for the cost estimate to be traced back to and verified against its sources and explain the variances between planned and actual costs.

---

[22]We previously reported that the CMP office changed its budget reporting by combining its cost estimates for contingency and escalation. While both categories account for uncertainties, combining them can reduce the transparency of how these funds are being used.

[23]Over the years, we have reported that many programs overrun their budgets due, in part, to difficulties estimating program costs. While not an exact comparison, we reported that cost estimates for the Capital Visitor Center rose from $303.5 million in 2003 to $621 million in 2007 due to uncertainties related to the preliminary nature of the design work, the unknown scope of pre-construction requirements, and security adjustments to the design after the events of September 11, 2001.

[24]GAO-09-3SP.

These best practices may also help address some of the concerns raised by the UN General Assembly regarding the CMP's cost estimates. For example, using the best practices associated with a well-documented cost estimate can improve an estimate's transparency, by capturing in writing such things as the source of the data used, the calculations performed, and the rationale for choosing particular estimating methods. Table 6 shows how the concerns of the UN General Assembly regarding the CMP's cost estimates could be addressed by using our best practices, as well as the potential benefits of this approach.

Table 6: UN General Assembly Concerns Regarding the CMP's Cost Estimates as Related to Best Practices

Concern	Related best practice	Specific element of best practice	Potential benefit
Lack of transparency and timely information on the budget, forecasts, and projected cost overruns	Comprehensive	Document all cost-influencing ground rules and assumptions in the estimate.	Clearly documenting the ground rules and assumptions of a cost estimate provides a basis for areas of potential risk to be resolved.
	Accurate	Document, explain, and review the variances between planned and actual costs.	Properly explaining the variance between planned and actual costs allows estimators to determine the quality of their estimates and how the project has changed over time.
		Regularly update the cost estimate to reflect significant changes in the program so that it always reflects current status.	Updating an estimate allows estimators to analyze changes in program costs and provide decision makers with accurate information for assessing alternative decisions.
Lack of transparency and timely information on risks	Credible	Conduct a risk and uncertainty analysis that quantifies the imperfectly understood risk and identify these effects of changing key cost driver assumptions and factors.	A risk and uncertainty analysis can help managers determine a level of funding to hold in reserve to cover costs resulting from uncertainties.
Lack of clarity regarding the renovation of the Library and South Annex	Well-documented	Describe in sufficient detail the calculations performed and the estimating methodology used to derive each element's cost in the documentation.	Documentation can help validate and defend a cost estimate.

Source: GAO analysis of UN General Assembly resolution A/RES/66/258 and GAO *Cost Estimating and Assessment Guide*, GAO-09-3SP.

CMP officials told us that they plan to present the additional information requested by the UN General Assembly in fall 2012. Applying these best practices, as appropriate, may help the CMP office as it prepares updated cost materials.

UN Considering Consolidation Building to Address UN Office Space Needs, but a Cost Estimate Has Not Been Completed

To address its future office space needs, the UN is considering the option of a new building that would be separate from the CMP, but it does not have an estimate of the project's costs. The UN estimates that its office space needs will exceed the capacity of its current real estate portfolio by 2023, due primarily to expiring leases. As a potential solution, the City and State of New York have proposed the construction of a new office building, to be located across the street from UN headquarters, known as the consolidation building. This proposal requires UN General Assembly approval, but the UN has not entered into any formal agreements regarding the building and the current lack of a cost estimate makes its cost implications for the UN and its member states unclear. We have previously reported that reliable cost estimates are critical to program success, including informed resource investments.

The UN Anticipates Office Space Needs at Its Headquarters Will Exceed Capacity by 2023

In September 2011, the Office of the Secretary-General completed a report on future office space accommodation needs for UN headquarters. The study estimates that, as of 2014, its real estate portfolio in New York will consist of approximately 3.4 million square feet of space—about 39 percent owned and 61 percent leased.[25] The UN headquarters campus comprises the majority of the UN's owned space, with office space in the Secretariat Building, Conference Building, Library, basements, and General Assembly Building. The UN also leases space in various locations around its headquarters campus to accommodate staff that cannot be housed in its owned space.[26]

However, due to the combination of expiring leases and estimated staff growth, the Secretary-General's report estimates that by 2023 the UN's office space needs will exceed the capacity of the owned and leased buildings currently in its real estate portfolio. Leases for the UN's two largest leased office spaces expire at the end of March 2018, with options to extend to the end of March 2023, but no renewal options beyond that date. The UN Development Corporation (UNDC)—a public benefit

---

[25]The UN chose the year 2014 as the starting point for its long-term space needs assessment. According to the UN, the organization plans to vacate temporary swing spaces leased for the CMP prior to 2014. Therefore, it did not include these leased spaces in its assessment.

[26]The CMP plans to renovate office space owned by the UN on its headquarters campus. However, even after the UN completes the renovation of these buildings, it will still require additional office space to accommodate its headquarters staff.

corporation of the State of New York whose mission is to provide office space and other facilities to help meet the current and future space needs of the UN—constructed these buildings in 1976 for use by the UN. The buildings provide approximately 670,000 square feet of office space, housing about 2,500 staff. The UN currently leases these buildings at below-market rates. According to the Secretary-General's report, renegotiating the leases beyond 2023 would likely result in lease rates set at market rates, rather than the favorable below-market rates currently enjoyed by the UN.[27] Additionally, the Secretary-General's report projects that headquarters staff levels will increase from 10,711 in 2014 to 11,911 in 2023. Using the report's estimate that each additional staff person requires an additional 250 square feet of space per person, this increase will require an additional 300,000 square feet of office space. We have not independently verified the report's per person space estimate. However, in October 2011, the UN's Advisory Committee on Administrative and Budgetary Questions found that a more in-depth and comprehensive analysis of the factors affecting the UN's space requirements was needed.

Consolidation Building Proposed as an Option to Address UN Long-Term Office Space Needs

The City and State of New York have initiated a proposal to construct a new office building—known as the consolidation building—that could help the UN address some of its long-term office space needs, but the UN has not entered into any agreements on the proposal. In July 2011, the Governor of the State of New York signed legislation authorizing the City of New York to transfer parkland to UNDC to construct a new office building for the UN as large as 900,000 square feet and located across the street from UN headquarters. In October 2011, key officials of the City and State of New York entered into a memorandum of understanding (MOU) regarding the consolidation building. The MOU, to which UNDC consented, obligates UNDC to specific actions, including initial funding for and issuance of bonds to finance the project. Per the MOU, the property will not convey to the UN until UNDC and UN reach agreement on the terms, with a deadline of December 31, 2015. According to UNDC officials, they would like to receive agreement from the UN by early 2014.

---

[27]The UN has estimated that the market rates for the space effective in 2023 would be $77 per square foot.

UN officials told us that they were informed of the MOU by UNDC officials shortly before it was finalized and signed, but have not entered into a formal agreement regarding the consolidation building. UN officials stated that they did not see the MOU prior to the City and State of New York signing it in October 2011 and therefore had no input to the document. Moreover, while the UN is not a party to the MOU, the document contains requirements to which the UN must agree for the consolidation building to move forward. For example, the UN would have to agree to lease the new office building from UNDC, potentially in a lease-to-own or similar arrangement. UN officials expressed concern that some of the terms of the MOU could increase costs and risks to the UN. For instance, according to UN officials, leasing the building would likely require the UN to pay an amount roughly equivalent to the bonds issued by UNDC to design and construct the consolidation building.[28] UN officials told us that since they will not know the potential lease costs until the bonds are issued, they would like the option to opt out of the project upon review of the potential costs. Additionally, according to the MOU, as a condition of agreeing to lease the consolidation building, the UN would have to extend the leases at two of its largest leased spaces at increased rental rates and with additional costs. For instance, according to the terms of the UN's current lease, its rates will increase from $27.50 per square foot (about $18.2 million per year) to $30 per square foot (about $19.8 million per year) if the organization exercises the option to extend its lease from 2018 to 2023. However, according to UN officials, under the MOU, the UN would have to extend the leases from 2018 to 2023 and its rates could rise to market rates, estimated by the UN to be approximately $77 per square foot. Additional costs include an amount equal to real estate taxes attributable to the space, which UN officials said was not originally included in the lease renewal terms. Finally, UN officials cited concerns related to "risk sharing" in the proposal. Specifically, officials expressed concern that the proposal places the entire risk for the cost of the project on the UN, rather than sharing the risk between the UN and UNDC. UN officials told us that they continue to discuss the consolidation building and its potential costs with UNDC officials. However, as of June 2012, the UN had not entered into a formal agreement regarding the consolidation building.

---

[28] UN officials told us the MOU may also require them to cover $73 million in funds used to acquire the land on which to construct the consolidation building.

UN officials told us that the UN General Assembly's Fifth Committee, which reviews administrative and budgetary issues, plans to discuss options related to the consolidation building at its fall 2012 session.

Cost Estimate for the Consolidation Building Not Completed

While the UN has held discussions with UNDC, neither organization has completed a cost estimate for the consolidation building. In October 2011, the UN's Advisory Committee on Administrative and Budgetary Questions reviewed the Secretary General's office space study. The committee noted that future UN space requirements could vary significantly depending on the underlying assumptions for estimating staff growth and space allowance per person, as well as alternative workplace policies. The committee also concluded that it was not fully convinced of the assumptions used to establish the baseline estimates of the UN's future office space requirements. Moreover, the committee stated its desire to compare all potential options for future office space accommodation, and recommended that the Secretary-General complete a detailed cost analysis of the consolidation building comparing the potential cost of the building to other options.

We have previously reported that a reliable cost estimate is critical to the success of any program. Such an estimate provides the basis for informed investment decision making, realistic budget formulation and program resourcing, meaningful progress measurement, proactive course correction when warranted, and accountability for results. While the UN's recommendations did not clarify what to include in the cost estimate for the consolidation building, our research has identified a number of best practices that form the basis of effective program cost estimating and should result in reliable and valid cost estimates that management can use for making informed decisions. As noted earlier, a high-quality and reliable cost estimate is comprehensive, well-documented, accurate, and credible. For example, a comprehensive cost estimate should include all life-cycle costs of a project, document all cost-influencing ground rules and assumptions affecting the estimate, and completely define the program and its schedule, among other best practices. See table 7 for the best practices associated with a high-quality and reliable cost estimate.

Table 7: Best Practices for a High-Quality and Reliable Cost Estimate

Best Practice	Best practice description
Comprehensive	A comprehensive cost estimate should include costs of the program over its full life cycle, provide a level of detail appropriate to ensure that cost elements are neither omitted nor double-counted, and document all cost-influencing ground rules and assumptions.
Well-documented	A well-documented cost estimate should capture in writing such things as the source and significance of the data used, the calculations performed and their results, and the rationale for choosing a particular estimating method. A well-documented estimate can be traced back to and verified against sources and should be reviewed and accepted by management.
Accurate	An accurate cost estimate should be, among other things, unbiased, not overly conservative or optimistic, based on historical data reflecting most likely costs, and adjusted properly for inflation. An accurate estimate should be updated regularly to reflect the current status, such as material changes in and actual cost experiences of the program, and steps should be taken to minimize mathematical mistakes. Further, variances between planned and actual costs should be documented, explained, and reviewed.
Credible	The cost estimates should discuss any limitations of the analysis because of uncertainty, or biases surrounding data or assumptions. Risk and uncertainty analysis should be performed to determine the level of risk associated with the estimate. Further, the estimate's results should be cross-checked against an independent estimate.

Source: GAO analysis based on the GAO *Cost Estimating and Assessment Guide*, GAO-09-3SP.

UN officials told us that they plan to conduct a cost analysis of the consolidation building. However, as of June 2012, the UN had not completed such an estimate. A cost estimate using our best practices could assist the UN in predicting the level of confidence in meeting the project's budget by quantifying risks and uncertainties associated with the project. Such an estimate gives decision makers perspective on the potential variability of the estimate, should facts, circumstances, and assumptions change. We have found that, without the ability to generate reliable cost estimates, projects risk experiencing cost overruns, missed deadlines, and performance shortfalls. As a result, absent a completed cost estimate for the consolidation building, the potential cost implications for the UN and its member states are not clear.

Conclusions

As the CMP nears completion of the renovations of the Secretariat and Conference Buildings, the project is estimated to be approximately $430 million over budget and risks remain as some renovations have yet to begin. Financing options exist to address a portion of the projected cost overrun; however, the United States and other UN member states may be asked to provide an additional assessment to finance the remainder. Aware of this risk, the UN General Assembly has requested that the CMP produce additional reporting on its costs. We have found that the best practices of developing high-quality and reliable cost estimates help inform decisions to manage capital projects effectively. Given the cost overruns and challenges of the CMP, as well as the risks and unknown costs associated with the UN's potential consolidation building project, these practices should be used to enhance the CMP's future cost estimates and to develop cost estimates of prospective projects to address the UN's long-term space needs. Such an approach would likely improve the quality and reliability of cost information provided to the UN and its member states, as well as help decision makers evaluate costs and risks associated with these projects.

Recommendations for Executive Action

To improve the quality and reliability of information provided to the UN and its member states, we recommend that the Secretary of State and U.S. Permanent Representative to the United Nations work with other member states to take the following two actions:

1. Direct the CMP office to implement, as appropriate, GAO's best practices for cost estimation when it updates information on CMP costs.

2. Direct the UN to ensure the development of a cost estimate for the consolidation building utilizing GAO's best practices for cost estimation.

Agency Comments and Our Evaluation

We provided a copy of this report to State and the UN for review and comment. State and the UN provided written comments, which are reproduced in appendixes III and IV, and technical comments, which we have incorporated as appropriate.

State concurred with our recommendations and expressed its concern that projected cost overruns of the CMP had grown to approximately $430 million. State also noted that it is not actively considering the use of TEF credits to address a U.S. share of a potential additional assessment for the CMP since member states have yet to decide on proposed funding options to address cost overruns. However, given that the estimated cost overruns of the CMP would still be approximately $212.7 million even if the UN approves the use of proposed funding sources, we maintain that an additional member assessment may be needed and that TEF credits attributable to the United States are a possible source of funding such an assessment.

The UN noted that our report was an accurate assessment of the status of the CMP and that it provided constructive recommendations.

We are sending copies of this report to interested congressional committees, the Secretary of State, the U.S. Mission to the United Nations, and the UN. In addition, the report is available at no charge on the GAO website at http://www.gao.gov.

If you or your staff have any questions about this report, please contact Thomas Melito at (202) 512-9601 or melitot@gao.gov, or David Wise at David Wise, (202) 512-2834 or wised@gao.gov. Contact points for our Offices of Congressional Relations and Public Affairs may be found on the last page of this report. GAO staff who made key contributions to this report are listed in appendix V.

Thomas Melito
Director, International Affairs and Trade

David Wise
Director, Physical Infrastructure Issues

Appendix I: Objectives, Scope, and Methodology

This report provides information on the progress of the United Nations (UN) Capital Master Plan (CMP) and the status of the UN consolidation building. Specifically, we examine (1) the extent to which the CMP is meeting its planned renovation scope, schedule, and budget; (2) the UN General Assembly's evaluation of CMP cost estimates; and (3) the status of the UN consolidation building project.

To address our objectives, we reviewed and analyzed relevant planning, schedule, and budget documents related to the CMP, as well as relevant planning and legal documents related to the consolidation building. Additionally, we discussed the progress, plans, risks, and costs of the CMP and consolidation building project with officials from the Department of State's (State) Bureau of International Organizations, the U.S. Mission to the UN, New York City, and UN offices, including the CMP office and Central Support Services. We also discussed efforts related to the consolidation building project with the UN Development Corporation, a public benefit corporation created to develop and operate office space for the benefit of the UN. We focused on these agencies because they are involved in the efforts of the CMP and the UN consolidation building project.

To examine the extent to which the CMP is meeting its planned renovation scope, schedule, and budget, we analyzed documents such as CMP annual reports, UN Board of Auditors reports on the CMP, and UN General Assembly resolutions. We compared current planned renovation scope, projected completion dates, and cost estimates with previously reported scope, schedule, and budget projections. For our baseline comparison, we referred to UN General Assembly resolutions that approved the planned renovation scope and schedule from accelerated strategy IV in 2007 and the $1.88 billion budget for the CMP in 2006. Further, we examined other relevant CMP documentation, including information on risk assessments, monthly reports, and procurement information. To understand the project's cost estimates, we examined materials provided by the CMP office to the UN General Assembly's Fifth Committee documenting the project's financial condition as of February 2012, and analyzed reports on CMP progress and associated costs produced by the Advisory Committee on Administrative and Budgetary Questions and the Program Planning and Budget Division. We also discussed these costs and the CMP's integrated master schedule with CMP officials. To understand options for funding projected CMP cost overruns, we reviewed UN Financial Rules and Regulations, UN Financial Report and Audited Financial Statements, and relevant congressional requirements in Appropriations Law, such as the

Consolidated Appropriations Act of 2012. Further, we held discussions with officials from the CMP office, the UN Program Planning and Budget Division, UN Board of Auditors, and State's Bureau of International Organizations to understand the various options that the United States could utilize to finance its portion of projected CMP cost overruns. We also traveled to New York City, New York, to tour the renovation sites and observe the progress of the CMP. During these visits, we met with officials from the CMP office, various UN departments—Program Planning and Budget Division, Board of Auditors, Office of Internal Oversight Services—and the U.S. Mission to the UN to discuss the ways in which the CMP is meeting its planned renovation scope, schedule, and budget.

To examine the UN General Assembly's evaluation of CMP cost estimates, we reviewed and analyzed documents provided by the CMP office to the UN General Assembly's Fifth Committee describing the project's financial condition as of February 2012, UN General Assembly resolution 66/258 issued in April 2012, the 2011 CMP annual report proposing financing options, and the Advisory Committee on Administrative and Budgetary Questions report A/66/7/Add.11 on costs of the CMP. Further, we analyzed the extent to which best practices for cost estimating from our *Cost Estimating and Assessment Guide* could potentially address concerns raised by the UN General Assembly with regard to the cost information provided by the CMP office. We did not conduct a full assessment of the CMP's February 2012 cost estimates, as (a) the estimates were updated projections provided in response to questions from the UN General Assembly's Fifth Committee during briefings, rather than comprehensive cost estimates; and (b) the CMP office intends to provide a full report on the project's costs, including new cost estimates, in fall 2012. Although we did not audit the CMP cost data and are not expressing an opinion on them, based on our examination of the documents received and our discussions with cognizant officials, we concluded that the data were sufficiently reliable for the purposes of this engagement. We also held discussions with officials from the CMP office, UN Program Planning and Budget Division, UN Board of Auditors, and the U.S. Mission to the UN on a number of factors affecting CMP cost estimates.

To examine the status of the UN consolidation project, we analyzed the memorandum of understanding (MOU) signed between the City and State of New York to identify actions required by the MOU. Additionally, we reviewed UN documents such as the Secretary-General's *Feasibility Study on the United Nations Headquarters Accommodation Needs 2014-*

2034 and a related report by the Advisory Committee on Administrative and Budgetary Questions to understand the UN's long-term office space needs. We conducted interviews with officials from New York City, the UN Development Corporation, and the UN regarding negotiations related to the consolidation building and lease costs for buildings potentially affected. Further, we reviewed how our best practices for cost estimating could provide insight on potential project costs to inform UN decision making.

We conducted our work from January 2012 to July 2012 in accordance with generally accepted government auditing standards. Those standards require that we plan and perform our work to obtain sufficient, appropriate evidence to provide a reasonable basis for our findings and conclusions based on our objectives. We believe that the evidence obtained provides a reasonable basis for our findings and conclusions based on our objectives.

Appendix II: UN Tax Equalization Fund

The United States annually pays assessed contributions to the UN General Fund to support the UN's programs and activities. One of these activities is a staff assessment, which is an amount deducted from the gross pay of all UN employees and used to fund the UN Tax Equalization Fund (TEF). The UN established the TEF to equalize the net pay of all UN staff members whatever their national tax obligations. While most UN employees are exempt from paying income tax on their UN earnings in their home country, some UN employees, including U.S. nationals, are not. For member states that levy income taxes on the earnings of UN employees, such as the United States, contributions to the TEF are first used to reimburse UN employees for the taxes they paid on their UN income.[1] Unused TEF credits remain as a balance in a member state's TEF account.

The UN reports TEF credits on a biennial basis. According to U.S. and UN officials, various factors, such as modifications in U.S. tax laws or changes in the number of U.S. employees at the UN, can result in TEF credits or debits in a member state's account. As shown in table 8, credits in the TEF attributable to the United States and reported by the UN rose by over $160 million between 2001 and 2009—from $17.6 million to $179 million.

---

[1]Member states that do not levy income taxes on the earnings of UN employees receive TEF credits as an offset against their mandatory UN assessments.

Table 8: Credits in the UN Tax Equalization Fund Attributable to the United States, 2001-2009, as Reported by the UN

Dollars in millions

Biennium ending	Amount of credits	Change from previous biennium[a]
December 31, 2001	$17.6	
December 31, 2003	$50.8	$33.2
December 31, 2005	$97.3	$46.5
December 31, 2007	$126.0	$28.7
December 31, 2009	$179.0	$53.0

Source: GAO analysis of UN Board of Auditors, Financial Report and Audited Financial Statements.

[a]This table shows changes from previous biennium beginning with 2003.

If a member state's TEF account has a balance, the Financial Rules and Regulations of the UN state that such a balance shall be credited against the mandatory assessed contributions due from that member state the following year.[2] However, notwithstanding UN financial regulations that TEF credits should be applied toward a member state's assessed contributions, TEF credits attributable to the United States were applied to fund enhanced security upgrades to the CMP. In October 2010, the UN requested State's endorsement of the use of up to $100 million of TEF credits accrued in prior years. In a January 2011 letter to the UN, State acknowledged the UN's use of up to $100 million in U.S. TEF credits described as "attributable to annual U.S. regular budget contributions" to fund the enhanced security upgrades.[3]

This transaction differs from previous uses of TEF credits. For example, State has previously requested that TEF credits be applied toward assessed contributions for the UN. Specifically, we reported that in 1997 the U.S. payment for its regular budget assessment included a $27.3

---

[2]UN Regulation 4.12. United Nations, *Financial Regulations and Rules of the United Nations,* ST/SGB/2003/7. Mandatory assessed contributions include those in the UN regular budget, peacekeeping operation accounts, and international criminal tribunal accounts.

[3]State also informed Congress of this pending transaction in letters sent in December 2010.

million credit from surplus funds in the TEF.[4] UN officials confirmed that TEF credits attributable to the United States were previously applied toward U.S. assessed contributions; however, they noted that in the case of the enhanced security upgrades the credits were used for a different purpose.

[4]GAO, *United Nations: Financial Issues and U.S. Arrears,* GAO/NSIAD-98-201BR, (Washington, D.C.: June 18, 1998).

Appendix III: Comments from the Department of State

Note: GAO comments supplementing those in the report appear at the end of this appendix.

United States Department of State
Comptroller
1969 Dyess Avenue
Charleston, SC 29405

JUL 0 9 2012

Dr. Loren Yager
Managing Director
International Affairs and Trade
Government Accountability Office
441 G Street, N.W.
Washington, D.C. 20548-0001

Dear Dr. Yager:

We appreciate the opportunity to review your draft report,
"UN RENOVATIONS: Use of Best Practices Could Enhance Future Cost
Estimates" GAO Job Code 320892.

The enclosed Department of State comments are provided for
incorporation with this letter as an appendix to the final report.

If you have any questions concerning this response, please contact
Ted Faris, Program Analyst, Bureau of International Organization Affairs
at (202) 736-4823.

Sincerely,

James L. Millette

cc: GAO – David J. Wise
        IO – Esther D. Brimmer
        State/OIG – Evelyn Klemstine

Department of State Comments on GAO Draft Report

UN Renovations: Use of Best Practices Could Enhance Future Cost Estimates
(GAO-12-795; GAO Code 320892)

Thank you for the opportunity to comment on the draft report entitled *UN Renovations: Use of Best Practices Could Enhance Future Cost Estimates*. The Department of State welcomes the report and concurs with the recommendation that the Capital Master Plan (CMP) Office should implement best practices for cost estimation contained in GAO's *Cost Estimating and Assessment Guide*, to the extent practical.

The Department was shocked to learn in March that the cost overrun had grown so significantly. The U.S. mission to the UN joined with other delegations in expressing concern to the CMP Office about the increase in the overrun. UN member states generally shared this concern and requested the Secretary General, through a General Assembly resolution, to ensure completion of the project within the approved budget. The General Assembly resolution also urgently requested a report on measures taken to address the risks that the Board of Auditors identified and an in-depth technical construction audit by the Office of Internal Oversight Services addressing the circumstances that led to the $430 million cost overrun.

See comment 1.

The draft report raises the possibility of the UN applying Tax Equalization Fund credits attributable to the United States to address the U.S. share of a potential additional assessment for the CMP. The Department is not actively considering this possibility, given that member states have conveyed to the Secretary-General that the project should proceed within the previously approved level of funding, and given that member states have not yet decided on proposals by the CMP Office to use other existing sources of funding, such as the working capital fund and interest earnings, to support the project.

See comment 2.

The Department acknowledges that a cost estimate for the consolidation building has not yet been provided. However, potential construction of the consolidation building is not part of the Capital Master Plan. While the Department concurs that a sound cost estimate is important for the United States and other member states to decide whether the proposed construction of the consolidation building makes sound economic sense, we question the association made in the report between the CMP major renovation project and the proposed new construction of the consolidation building, which would not be directly managed by the UN.

The following are GAO's comments on State's letter dated July 9, 2012.

GAO Comments

1. We maintain that an additional member assessment may be needed and that Tax Equalization Fund credits attributable to the United States remain a possible source of funding for such an assessment. Given the Capital Master Plan's (CMP) projected cost overruns of approximately $430 million, even if the United Nations (UN) General Assembly approves the use of proposed funding sources and reductions in planned renovations, the estimated cost overruns of the project would still be $212.7 million. In the event of cost escalations over the approved budget of the CMP, the UN General Assembly decided that member states would be subject to a further assessment. The U.S. share of any future assessment would be 22 percent.

2. Our report makes clear that the CMP project is separate from the consolidation building proposal. However, we maintain that regardless of whether the UN directly manages the construction of the consolidation building, a sound cost estimate should be developed as the UN will be responsible for financing the building should it agree to its construction.

Appendix IV: Comments from the United Nations

United Nations   Nations Unies

HEADQUARTERS · SIEGE   NEW YORK, NY 10017
TEL.: 1 (212) 963.1889 · FAX: 1 (917) 367.5377

17 July 2012

Dear Mr. Melito and Mr. Wise:

Thank you very much for your electronic communication dated 18 June 2012 in which you requested our comments on GAO's draft report on the Capital Master Plan.

In summary, the draft GAO report is an accurate assessment of the status of the project, and provides constructive recommendations. Upon receipt of your draft report, staff members from the Office of the Capital Master Plan were in contact with members of your team and provided several suggestions regarding the report. I understand your team will be taking these suggestions into account as you finalize your report.

As you are aware, the Tenth Annual Progress Report of the Secretary-General on the Capital Master Plan is presently under preparation, and will be submitted for consideration by the General Assembly in their fall session. That report will contain updated information on the Capital Master Plan.

I wish to extend my appreciation to your team for their continued courtesy and professionalism.

Sincerely,

Michael Adlerstein
Assistant Secretary-General and
Executive Director
Capital Master Plan

Mr. Thomas Melito, Director, International Affairs and Trade
Mr. David Wise, Director, Physical Infrastructure Issues
U.S. Government Accountability Office
Washington, DC

Appendix V: GAO Contacts and Staff Acknowledgments

GAO Contacts	Thomas Melito, Director, International Affairs and Trade, (202) 512-9601 or melitot@gao.gov David Wise, Director, Physical Infrastructure Issues, (202) 512-2834 or wised@gao.gov
Staff Acknowledgments	In addition to the contacts named above, Maria Edelstein, Assistant Director; Biza Repko; Adam Yu; Mark Dowling; Debbie J. Chung; Jason Lee; and Karen Richey made key contributions to this report. Joshua Ormond provided technical assistance.

Related GAO Products

United Nations: Renovation Still Scheduled for Completion in 2013, but Risks to Its Schedule and Cost Remain. GAO-09-870R. (Washington, D.C.: July 30, 2009).

United Nations: Renovation Schedule Accelerated after Delays, but Risks Remain in Key Areas. GAO-08-513R. (Washington, D.C.: April 9, 2008).

Update on the United Nations' Capital Master Plan. GAO-07-414R. (Washington, D.C.: February 15, 2007).

United Nations: Renovation Planning Follows Industry Practices, but Procurement and Oversight Could Present Challenges. GAO-07-31. (Washington, D.C.: November 16, 2006).

United Nations: Early Renovation Planning Reasonable, but Additional Management Controls and Oversight Will Be Needed. GAO-03-566. (Washington, D.C.: May 30, 2003).

United Nations: Planning for Headquarters Renovation is Reasonable; United States Needs to Decide Whether to Support Work. GAO-01-788. (Washington, D.C.: June 15, 2001).

GAO's Mission	The Government Accountability Office, the audit, evaluation, and investigative arm of Congress, exists to support Congress in meeting its constitutional responsibilities and to help improve the performance and accountability of the federal government for the American people. GAO examines the use of public funds; evaluates federal programs and policies; and provides analyses, recommendations, and other assistance to help Congress make informed oversight, policy, and funding decisions. GAO's commitment to good government is reflected in its core values of accountability, integrity, and reliability.
Obtaining Copies of GAO Reports and Testimony	The fastest and easiest way to obtain copies of GAO documents at no cost is through GAO's website (www.gao.gov). Each weekday afternoon, GAO posts on its website newly released reports, testimony, and correspondence. To have GAO e-mail you a list of newly posted products, go to www.gao.gov and select "E-mail Updates."
Order by Phone	The price of each GAO publication reflects GAO's actual cost of production and distribution and depends on the number of pages in the publication and whether the publication is printed in color or black and white. Pricing and ordering information is posted on GAO's website, http://www.gao.gov/ordering.htm. Place orders by calling (202) 512-6000, toll free (866) 801-7077, or TDD (202) 512-2537. Orders may be paid for using American Express, Discover Card, MasterCard, Visa, check, or money order. Call for additional information.
Connect with GAO	Connect with GAO on Facebook, Flickr, Twitter, and YouTube. Subscribe to our RSS Feeds or E-mail Updates. Listen to our Podcasts. Visit GAO on the web at www.gao.gov.
To Report Fraud, Waste, and Abuse in Federal Programs	Contact: Website: www.gao.gov/fraudnet/fraudnet.htm E-mail: fraudnet@gao.gov Automated answering system: (800) 424-5454 or (202) 512-7470
Congressional Relations	Katherine Siggerud, Managing Director, siggerudk@gao.gov, (202) 512-4400, U.S. Government Accountability Office, 441 G Street NW, Room 7125, Washington, DC 20548
Public Affairs	Chuck Young, Managing Director, youngc1@gao.gov, (202) 512-4800 U.S. Government Accountability Office, 441 G Street NW, Room 7149 Washington, DC 20548

Please Print on Recycled Paper.

www.ingramcontent.com/pod-product-compliance
Lightning Source LLC
Chambersburg PA
CBHW080918290526
45795CB00007BA/2564